This Coloring Book Belongs To

____

This Is How I Roll

This Is
How I Roll

I Just Freaking
love Hamsters,
Ok?

I Just Freaking
love Hamsters,
Ok?

Sawdust Is
My Glitter

Sawdust Is
My Glitter

Life Is Better
With Hamsters

Life Is Better
With Hamsters

Positive
Vibes

Positive
Vibes

Hold Me
Closer Tiny
Hamster

Hold Me
Closer Tiny
Hamster

Enjoy
The Little
Things

Enjoy
The Little
Things

Made in the USA
Las Vegas, NV
13 January 2024

84317912R00024